Breath State

Robert Pudlock

Copyright

Introduction: Why This Book Exists

You can have the right method and still fail to execute it.

This is one of the most common and least understood performance problems in modern work.

People adopt proven systems, set goals, build routines, and install accountability.

For a while, progress appears real.

Then output degrades, recovery stops working, and effort rises as results fall.

Most advice interprets this as a motivation problem, a discipline issue, or a planning error.

This book argues something more precise:

The failure often happens because state is misread, sequence is violated, and unresolved loops remain active.

Breath State is a diagnostic framework for this problem.

It is not a productivity method.

It is not a therapeutic model.

It does not replace execution systems.

It sits upstream of them.

The framework is built on three states:

- Inhale: internal capacity accumulation

- Pause: neutral suspension between directional states

- Exhale: external expression of capacity

Loop integrity tracks whether Inhale and Exhale resolve cleanly:

- closed loop: no residual claim remains active

- open loop: unresolved demand continues to tax attention and energy

Your practical gain from this book is simple:

you will diagnose state and loop status before selecting action.

That one shift changes everything downstream.

Chapter 1 - Why Reliable People Still Break Their Systems

If you are reading this, you are probably not careless.

You are probably not unserious.

You may even be the person others trust when things need to get done.

And yet, your system may still be failing in ways that do not make sense.

You run your calendar, but everything feels late.

You finish tasks, but nothing feels complete.

You take time off, but return tired.

You start strong, then leak momentum in ways you cannot explain.

When this happens, people usually receive one of three explanations:

- You need better discipline.

- You need a better method.

- You need to want it more.

All three explanations can be true in specific situations.

But they are often wrong in the situations that matter most.

Many high-capability people are already disciplined.

Many already use good methods.

Many already care deeply.

Their failure is not due to low intent.

It is due to high effort applied against structural conditions that do not support execution.

This chapter introduces the core thesis of the book:

Repeated system failure in capable people is frequently a state and sequence problem, not a character problem.

The Pattern Most People Miss

The modern performance stack is method-heavy and state-blind.

We teach prioritization, habit loops, accountability systems, sprint planning, OKRs, wellness routines, and productivity protocols.

These tools are not useless.

Some are excellent.

But almost all of them assume that a person can reliably enter and sustain the state required by the method at the moment the method calls for it.

That assumption fails often.

A planning system assumes availability for planning.

A focus protocol assumes availability for focus.

A recovery routine assumes the person can detach enough to recover.

An execution model assumes capacity can be externalized on demand.

When those assumptions are false, a good system appears to fail.

Then people stack more force on top.

The result is predictable:

- depletion gets interpreted as reluctance

- unresolved work gets interpreted as poor time management

- neutral integration gets interpreted as avoidance

The diagnosis is wrong, so the intervention is wrong, so the friction intensifies.

The Cost of a Moral Frame

A moral frame asks, "What is wrong with me?"

A structural frame asks, "What conditions are active, and what do they make predictable?"

This difference is not philosophical. It is operational.

If someone is in depleted Exhale and receives pressure to produce, output quality drops and recovery debt increases.

If someone is in open-loop Inhale and receives more learning inputs, congestion increases.

If someone is in true Pause and receives urgency prompts, integration is interrupted and downstream expression fragments.

None of those outcomes require a flawed personality.

They require a mismatched intervention.

Many professionals spend years trying to solve structural mismatch with moral effort.

They work harder on self-belief, self-talk, grit, discipline, and consistency while leaving loop status unresolved and transitions unprotected.

They are not weak.

They are over-optimized for effort and under-equipped for diagnosis.

Breath State™ is built to close that gap.

A Practical Reframe

Instead of asking:

"Why can't I stick to this system?"

Ask:

"What state am I in right now, and is my current loop closed?"

That question does three things immediately:

1. It lowers false self-judgment.

2. It increases intervention precision.

3. It reduces wasted force.

This is why the framework works as infrastructure.

Infrastructure does not tell you what goals to choose or which software to use. It tells you whether movement will be stable once you choose a method.

Signs You Are Dealing with Structure, Not Willpower

If these patterns are recurring, you are likely dealing with state/loop conditions:

- You can work hard for short bursts but cannot sustain clean output.

- "Rest" produces guilt or anxiety rather than restoration.

- Finished work still feels active and mentally sticky.

- New priorities do not displace old unresolved demands.

- You regularly feel urgent and stuck at the same time.

These are not random symptoms. They are coherent signals.

What This Book Will Do

Across the next chapters, you will learn to:

- identify Inhale, Pause, and Exhale with operational clarity

- detect open versus closed loops before they become costly

- choose interventions matched to state and loop status

- protect transitions so sequence remains stable under pressure

The objective is not maximal output.

The objective is sustainable output that does not destroy the system producing it.

Key Takeaways

- Capable people often fail from structural mismatch, not low character.

- Good methods fail when state assumptions are false.

- The first corrective move is diagnostic, not motivational.

- State-first execution reduces friction and wasted effort.

- State-first sequencing increases method reliability without adding complexity.

Chapter 2 - The Hidden Error - Method Before State

Most performance systems are designed to answer one of these questions:

- What should I do next?

- How should I prioritize?

- How should I track execution?

These are valid questions. They are just not first questions.

The first question is:

What condition is the system in right now?

Without that answer, methods become blunt instruments. The same tactic that is helpful in one condition becomes harmful in another:

- pushing for output helps in healthy Exhale but harms in depleted Exhale

- adding planning helps in coherent Inhale but worsens open-loop Inhale congestion

- encouraging "rest" helps after true depletion but fails when unresolved loops keep demand active

This is the hidden error of modern execution culture: method before state.

Upstream and Downstream

Think of performance as a layered stack.

Upstream layer:

- state (Inhale, Pause, Exhale)

- loop integrity (open or closed)

- transition quality (clean or contaminated)

Downstream layer:

- methods (planning systems, accountability routines, time blocks, cadence structures)

- tools (apps, dashboards, templates, workflows)

- behaviors (task execution, communication, delivery)

Downstream tools assume upstream stability.

When upstream conditions are unstable, downstream tools produce volatile outcomes.

This explains a common paradox:

the same person can "prove" that a method works on Monday and "prove" it fails on Thursday.

The method did not change. State conditions did.

Three Method Failures That Are Actually State Failures

Failure 1: Output Protocol Applied to Depleted Exhale

Observed problem: missed deadlines, avoidance, poor quality.

Common diagnosis: low discipline.

Structural diagnosis: output demands are being applied where capacity is depleted.

Result of wrong intervention:

more pressure, lower quality, deeper depletion.

Failure 2: Planning Protocol Applied to Open-Loop Inhale

Observed problem: lots of preparation, low decisive release.

Common diagnosis: perfectionism or fear.

Structural diagnosis: accumulation has no closure boundary and no expression trigger.

Result of wrong intervention:

more planning layers and higher cognitive load.

Failure 3: Recovery Protocol Applied to Unclosed Loops

Observed problem: rest does not restore.

Common diagnosis: person is "bad at relaxing."

Structural diagnosis: unresolved demand remains active during downtime.

Result of wrong intervention:

more rest time with persistent unrest.

Why the Misdiagnosis Persists

It persists because behavior is visible and state is not.

Managers can see missed outputs.

Peers can see reduced responsiveness.

Individuals can see tasks not moving.

But fewer people can see:

- whether the current state supports the demanded behavior

- whether unresolved loops are draining availability

- whether transitions are being compressed beyond stability

In the absence of diagnostic language, people default to moral language.

Moral language feels decisive, but it is low precision.

The Diagnostic Pre-Check

Before choosing any productivity or performance intervention, run this pre-check:

1. Which state is active now?

2. Is the dominant loop open or closed?

3. What transition boundary is currently weak?

4. Which method matches this condition?

Only after those four answers should you pick a tactic.

This sequence does not slow execution. It prevents expensive misfires.

Example: One Project, Two Different Diagnoses

Same situation:

A report is "almost done" for two weeks.

Diagnosis A (behavior-only):

"This person is procrastinating."

Intervention:

daily accountability pressure.

Likely outcome:

short bursts of forced output, persistent anxiety, low-quality finalization.

Diagnosis B (state-first):

"This is open-loop Exhale with unclear closure criteria."

Intervention:

define done threshold, force handoff point, create closure artifact.

Likely outcome:

clean release, loop closure, restored availability.

The second outcome is not better because it is kinder.

It is better because it is structurally accurate.

What "Method Before State" Looks Like in Organizations

At team level, this error appears as:

- adding process whenever friction appears

- interpreting unresolved demand as compliance failure

- treating transition time as inefficiency

- measuring activity volume instead of closure quality

At leadership level, it appears as:

- constant launch with weak retirement protocols

- no explicit "definition of done" at initiative boundaries

- pressure cycles that reward visible urgency over completed closure

These environments train people to hide open loops, not close them.

Practical Rule

Do not ask, "What system should we use?" until you ask, "What condition are we in?"

Method choice should be conditional.

Condition-blind methods create avoidable churn.

Key Takeaways

- Methods are downstream; state and loop integrity are upstream.

- A good method can fail when applied in the wrong condition.

- Most "discipline failures" are better explained as diagnostic failures.

Chapter 3 - The Three States

Inhale: Capacity Accumulation

Inhale is inward accumulation of internal capability.

Its effects are preparatory, not externally decisive.

Inhale may include:

- learning

- recovery

- planning

- rehearsal

- system setup

The test is directional, not emotional: does this increase internal readiness for later output?

Pause: Neutral Suspension

Pause is neutral non-directionality.

It is neither accumulation nor expression.

Pause is where integration and reorientation occur without forcing.

It is a structural boundary required for clean transition.

Exhale: Expression and Output

Exhale converts capacity into external consequence.

Exhale includes action that changes reality beyond the moment:

- publishing

- shipping

- presenting

- deciding

- delivering

Exhale is inherently costly: output spends accumulated capacity.

The Sequence Rule

Inhale -> Pause -> Exhale -> Pause -> Inhale ...

Violating sequence predicts failure:

- Exhale without Inhale -> depletion

- Inhale without Exhale -> congestion

- Remove Pause -> transition instability

Chapter 4 - Sequence Is a Constraint, Not a Preference

Modern tools compress time and erase boundaries. Messages arrive continuously. Workspaces stay open indefinitely. Feedback loops are instant.

This creates the illusion that transitions are optional.

They are not.

When boundary cues disappear externally, the requirement for transition moves inward. If that internal transition is not named and protected, the person experiences persistent low-grade friction and calls it normal.

It is not normal. It is unresolved sequence demand.

Chapter 5 - Friction as Signal, Not Character Failure

Friction is the experiential signal produced by mismatch or unresolved loops.

Treat friction as data, not identity.

Common misreads:

- "I am lazy" -> often depleted Exhale or genuine Pause

- "I am disorganized" -> often multiple open loops

- "I need more discipline" -> often wrong-state method application

Signal-first question:

What structural condition would generate this experience predictably?

Chapter 6 - Pause

Pause is frequently misunderstood because it looks quiet from the outside.

In environments optimized for visible productivity, quiet states are often interpreted as failure states.

That interpretation is expensive.

If you misclassify Pause as laziness, you prescribe pressure.

If you misclassify Pause as burnout, you prescribe recovery tactics that may not fit.

If you misclassify Pause as procrastination, you prescribe urgency.

In each case, the intervention can disrupt the very function Pause provides.

Core Definition

Pause is a state of neutral suspension characterized by absence of directional demand.

In Pause:

- the system is not actively accumulating capacity (Inhale)

- the system is not actively expressing capacity (Exhale)

- integration and reorientation occur without deliberate forcing

Pause is not "nothing happening."

Pause is "no directional demand applied."

This distinction matters.

Why Pause Is Structurally Necessary

Every directional system requires a neutral condition before reliable direction change.

Breath illustrates this physically: continuous inward pull without release fails, continuous outward push without restoration fails, and collapsed transition destabilizes both.

Human work follows the same constraint.

After expression, the system often needs a period where output has ended but new accumulation has not yet fully begun. After accumulation, the system may need neutral suspension before committing output. Pause is that boundary condition.

When Pause is removed, states bleed into one another:

- people try to recover while still outputting

- people attempt output while still unresolved from prior output

- people consume more input as a substitute for transition

The result is not speed. It is interference.

Five Operational Markers of Pause

Marker 1: Absence of Both Urgency and Depletion

There is no sharp demand to act now, and no inability to act if needed. This is a neutral readiness, not exhaustion and not drive.

Marker 2: Integration Rather Than Shutdown

People often report that something is "settling" in the background. They are not actively producing, but internal coherence is increasing.

Marker 3: Low Motivation Without Guilt

Drive may be low, but self-attack is also low. If guilt, pressure, or shame is dominant, Pause is less likely and blocked/open-loop states are more likely.

Marker 4: Future Orientation Without Compulsion

The next step feels possible and emerging, not threatening or forced. The person expects to re-engage, but not on panic terms.

Marker 5: External Mislabeling Risk

Observers often mistake Pause for disengagement because output temporarily drops. Behavior can look similar to avoidance from the outside while internal dynamics are very different.

Pause Versus Commonly Confused States

Pause vs Depleted Exhale

Depleted Exhale includes energy deficit and "cannot" signals.

Pause includes neutrality without depletion.

Pause vs Blocked Inhale

Blocked Inhale includes "should" pressure with inability to mobilize.

Pause includes little pressure and low conflict.

Pause vs Avoidance

Avoidance includes active conflict with required action.

Pause includes reduced internal conflict and greater integration.

Pause vs Recovery

Recovery rebuilds capacity and therefore belongs to Inhale.

Pause preserves neutrality and sequence integrity.

The Mislabeling Loop

One of the highest-cost mistakes is treating every low-output interval as pathology.

Path:

1. Person enters natural Pause after a demanding expression cycle.

2. Environment labels state as non-performance.

3. Pressure is applied to "reactivate."

4. Integration is interrupted.

5. Next expression phase begins fragmented.

6. Performance drops, which appears to confirm the original mislabel.

The label creates the outcome it predicts.

How to Protect Pause Without Drifting

Protecting Pause does not mean indefinite disengagement.

It means preserving the conditions that allow transition clarity.

Practical protection:

- Name the state explicitly.

- Reduce unnecessary external demand for immediate output.

- Use light boundary cues (end-of-cycle notes, low-load reflection, short reset walks).

- Watch for natural readiness signals rather than forced activation signals.

Readiness signals include:

- spontaneous interest in next steps

- return of coherent forward orientation

- reduced cognitive noise around prior cycle

Forced activation signals include:

- guilt spikes

- social pressure

- arbitrary calendar deadlines disconnected from state

Pause Decision Sequence (Applied)

Use this sequence whenever output is low and interpretation risk is high:

1. Is clear depletion present?

2. Is guilt/pressure/conflict dominant?

3. Does rest increase anxiety?

4. Is future orientation present without urgency?

5. Is there absence of urgency and depletion?

If 1-3 are mostly no and 4-5 are yes, Pause is likely.

Key Takeaways

- Pause is a neutral structural state, not a character failure.

- Pause supports transition integrity and integration.

- Mislabeling Pause often creates unnecessary fragmentation.

- Accurate naming is the highest-leverage first intervention.

Chapter 7 - Loop Integrity

Most people track tasks.

Few people track loop status.

That gap explains why many people look organized on paper and still feel fragmented in practice.

A task can be marked complete while remaining psychologically and operationally active. A project can remain unresolved even after significant work has been done. A person can take time off and stay internally tethered to unfinished obligations.

Loop integrity names this condition precisely.

Core Definition

Loop integrity is completion status within Inhale or Exhale.

A closed loop:

- resolves without residual claim on attention, energy, or future obligation

- permits clean transition to next state

An open loop:

- remains structurally incomplete

- continues to claim cognitive and emotional resources

- degrades transition quality and recovery quality

Pause has no loops.

Loops apply only to directional states.

Why Closure Is Relational

Closure is not only a property of the work artifact.

It is a property of the relationship between person and work.

Two people can touch the same project and have different loop statuses:

- For one person, handoff and acceptance close the loop.

- For another, unresolved ownership, standards, or ambiguity keep the loop open.

This is why "but it's done" often fails as reassurance.

Completion is necessary but not always sufficient for closure.

How Open Loops Generate Drag

Pathway 1: Cognitive Availability Tax

Unresolved demand remains active. Attention gets repeatedly pulled back. Working memory is consumed by maintenance rather than present-task engagement.

Pathway 2: Transition Interference

Open loops cross boundaries. You start new work but old unresolved work reactivates immediately. Neither receives full depth.

Pathway 3: Recovery Degradation

Rest periods fail because unresolved claims remain live. Physical rest occurs without full detachment, so restoration is partial.

These pathways are why people can sleep, vacation, and still feel unrecovered.

Operational Markers of Open Loops

Reliable signs include:

- intrusive return: unresolved items surface unbidden during unrelated activities

- anxious rest: downtime increases agitation

- rehearsal without execution: repeated planning loops without closure action

- fragmented new engagement: current work triggers old unresolved work

- defensive activation: neutral mentions of unresolved work trigger explanation/defense

No single marker is definitive.

Clusters of markers are diagnostically useful.

Closed- and Open-Loop States in Practice

Closed-Loop Inhale

Capacity-building activity concludes without pressure spillover.

Learning converts into readiness.

Transition remains clean.

Open-Loop Inhale

Accumulation continues without closure boundary.

Pressure builds toward expression, but expression is delayed or avoided.

The system feels congested.

Closed-Loop Exhale

Output is delivered or released with clear endpoint.

Residual obligation clears.

System can enter Pause or next Inhale coherently.

Open-Loop Exhale

Energy is spent, but unresolved demand remains.

Obligation persists after action.

Recovery quality declines.

The 9-Item Loop Integrity Check

Score YES/NO:

1. Does this work return to mind unbidden?

2. Do you repeatedly mentally rehearse completion without acting?

3. Can you not clearly state what happens next?

4. Does body tension rise when you think about this work?

5. Does sleep degrade before re-engagement?

6. Does rest increase anxiety?

7. Do you avoid people likely to ask about this work?

8. Does new work trigger this unfinished work?

9. Do neutral mentions trigger defensiveness?

Interpretation:

- 0-2 YES: likely closed

- 3-5 YES: partially open

- 6-9 YES: severely open, closure action required

Closure Mechanisms

To close loops, match the intervention to the failed mechanism:

- External boundary missing -> create handoff, deadline, or acceptance event.

- Internal release missing -> explicit declaration of sufficient completion.

- Scope sprawl missing closure -> version bifurcation (v1 closed, v2 backlog).

- Perfection loop active -> satisficing threshold with external validation.

Closure should be visible in artifacts:

- handoff message

- signed acceptance

- archived version

- completion note with explicit next-state boundary

If closure has no trace, the loop often reopens.

Common Errors in Loop Work

- Error: treating open loops as "just stress."

Fix: diagnose specific unresolved demand and closure mechanism.

- Error: adding planning layers to unresolved loops.

Fix: prioritize closure over optimization.

- Error: trying to recover without closure.

Fix: close or consciously release before extending recovery protocols.

Key Takeaways

- Loop integrity predicts availability more accurately than effort alone.

- "Done" and "closed" are different conditions.

- Open loops are structural load, not moral weakness.

- Explicit closure artifacts are high-leverage interventions.

Chapter 8 - Common Misdiagnoses and Category Errors

Misdiagnosis 1: Open-loop Exhale -> "time management problem"

Correction: closure mechanism, not another planning app.

Misdiagnosis 2: True Pause -> "procrastination"

Correction: accurate naming and boundary protection.

Misdiagnosis 3: Open-loop Inhale -> "lack of confidence"

Correction: forced application and expression boundary.

Misdiagnosis 4: Depleted Exhale -> "low ambition"

Correction: rebuild Inhale capacity before output push.

When diagnosis is wrong, intervention magnifies harm.

When diagnosis is accurate, intervention can be small and decisive.

Chapter 9 - The Pause Decision Sequence in Real Life

When output drops, most people jump straight to intervention.

That is usually too early.

Start with diagnosis.

The Pause Decision Sequence is designed for one high-risk moment:

low-output periods that can be mistaken for laziness, burnout, or avoidance.

Used correctly, this sequence prevents expensive misclassification.

The Sequence

1. Is clear depletion present?

2. Is guilt, internal pressure, or conflict dominant?

3. Does downtime increase anxiety?

4. Is future orientation present without urgency?

5. Is there absence of both urgency and depletion?

Interpretation:

- If 1 is yes -> likely depleted Exhale.

- If 2 is yes -> likely blocked state, not Pause.

- If 3 is yes -> likely open loops are active.

- If 4 and 5 are yes while 1-3 are no -> likely true Pause.

Why This Works

The sequence separates similar-looking states by internal mechanics, not surface behavior.

Surface behavior overlap:

- reduced output

- delayed initiation

- lower visible drive

Internal mechanics differ:

- depletion = low available capacity

- blockage = high internal conflict

- open loops = unresolved demand tax

- Pause = neutral suspension with integration

Intervention must follow mechanics, not appearance.

Daily Personal Use

Use this as a five-minute check during morning planning or end-of-day review.

Template:

- Current condition:

- Dominant marker:

- Likely classification:

- Next matched action:

Examples of matched actions:

- depleted Exhale -> reduce expression load, rebuild through targeted Inhale

- blocked state -> resolve pressure source, reduce internal contradiction

- open loops -> close one loop before adding new commitments

- true Pause -> protect boundary and avoid forced reactivation

Weekly Team Use

Leaders can integrate the sequence without adding heavy process.

Team protocol (15 minutes weekly):

1. Each person self-classifies current condition.

2. Team identifies where interventions are mismatched.

3. One boundary protection action is assigned per high-risk case.

Leadership language shift:

- replace "Why are you behind?" with "What condition are you operating from?"

- replace "Push through" with "What would restore clean sequence?"

This reduces blame and improves execution quality simultaneously.

Two Common Misuses

Misuse 1: Using "Pause" as a blanket justification for disengagement.

Correction: require marker-based classification, not preference-based claims.

Misuse 2: Forcing rapid diagnosis under high pressure without reflection.

Correction: use simple written prompts; decisions made too fast tend to default to moral frames.

Decision Boundaries

The sequence is not a mental health diagnostic instrument.

If severe or persistent distress is present, additional professional support may be appropriate.

Within the performance domain, the sequence is a triage tool:

it improves first-response accuracy.

Applied Example

Scenario:

A director reports low output for ten days after a major delivery.

Sequence:

1. Depletion? Mild only.

2. Guilt/conflict? Low.

3. Rest anxiety? Low.

4. Future orientation? Present ("I can see next quarter shape but don't need to force it today.")

5. Absence of urgency and depletion? Yes.

Classification:

Likely Pause.

Intervention:

protect two days of low-demand integration, then re-enter with scoped Inhale planning.

Outcome:

higher coherence and faster clean reactivation than pressure-based restart.

Key Takeaways

- The Pause sequence is a diagnostic filter, not a motivational script.

- Correct classification prevents high-cost intervention mismatch.

- Teams can adopt this with light cadence and improved manager language.

- Accurate naming often resolves friction before heavy intervention is required.

Chapter 10 - The Loop Integrity Check in Real Life

Most professionals track tasks by status:

not started, in progress, complete.

Loop integrity adds a missing status:

closed or open.

Without this distinction, people can finish many items and still carry unresolved demand load. The Loop Integrity Check is a practical way to make hidden load visible and actionable.

Weekly Loop Review Protocol

Run once per week, ideally before planning next-week commitments.

Step 1: Identify top three active demands.

- Choose items that produce the most cognitive return or emotional activation.

Step 2: Score each demand with the 9-item check.

- Use yes/no only.

- Do not overanalyze wording.

Step 3: Classify severity.

- 0-2 YES: likely closed or low risk

- 3-5 YES: partially open, closure recommended

- 6-9 YES: severely open, closure required before adding major new load

Step 4: Select one closure action per open loop.

- Match action to failed mechanism.

Step 5: Produce closure artifact.

- If no artifact exists, the loop is probably not closed.

Choosing the Right Closure Action

Match intervention to what is missing:

- Missing endpoint -> define done threshold in writing.

- Missing handoff -> schedule and execute formal transfer.

- Missing acceptance -> obtain explicit stakeholder confirmation.

- Missing release decision -> declare satisficing boundary.

- Excess future ideas -> bifurcate into current version + future backlog.

Wrong closure move example:

Adding another planning board to an item that already has clear plans but no release decision.

Right closure move:

Declare current version complete and hand off.

The "One Severe Loop" Rule

If one item scores 6+ YES, prioritize that closure first.

Reason:

Severe open loops produce disproportionate drag. Closing one high-load loop usually returns more capacity than optimizing ten low-load tasks.

This is one of the highest-leverage operational rules in the framework.

Team Implementation

A team can run loop review in 20 minutes:

1. Each member names one likely open loop.

2. Quick score and severity call.

3. One closure commitment per person.

4. Report closure artifacts at next check-in.

Team benefit:

- reduces invisible work-in-progress

- improves handoff reliability

- lowers background anxiety that is often mislabeled as "culture stress"

Common Failure Modes

Failure Mode 1: Confusing activity with closure.

High activity can coexist with open loops if no release boundary exists.

Failure Mode 2: Waiting for perfect completion.

Open loops stay open when "better" has no stopping rule.

Failure Mode 3: Emotional closure without operational closure.

Feeling better is useful; it is not sufficient if unresolved claim remains in workflow.

Failure Mode 4: Closing everything at once.

Loop closure is best done in sequence. Start with highest severity and move down.

Sample Weekly Worksheet

- Item:

- 9-item score:

- Severity band:

- Failed closure mechanism:

- Chosen closure action:

- Closure artifact:

- Recheck date:

If score does not improve on recheck, change mechanism assumption and choose a different closure intervention.

Applied Example

Scenario:

A product lead feels scattered despite "completing" many tickets.

Review:

- Item A (launch memo): score 7, missing acceptance from leadership.

- Item B (roadmap draft): score 4, missing done threshold.

- Item C (hiring rubric): score 2.

Actions:

- A: secure explicit acceptance in leadership review.

- B: declare v1 scope and archive v2 ideas.

- C: no action.

One week later:

- A drops to 2.

- B drops to 3.

- Subjective fragmentation significantly reduced.

Key Takeaways

- Loop status predicts available attention better than task status alone.

- Closure must be explicit and artifact-backed.

- One severe loop can distort an entire week of execution.

- Weekly loop review is a low-overhead, high-return operating rhythm.

Chapter 11 - Closing Loops by Context

Open loops do not all close the same way.

This is where many smart people lose traction. They apply one closure tactic to every domain, then conclude that loop work is inconsistent. It is not inconsistent. It is contextual.

The right question is not:

"How do I close loops in general?"

The right question is:

"What type of loop is this, and what closure mechanism fits this type?"

This chapter gives you context-specific closure patterns you can use immediately.

Closure Mechanism Map

Across domains, most successful closures rely on one or more of five mechanisms:

- external boundary (deadline, delivery, event)

- acceptance boundary (stakeholder sign-off)

- sufficiency boundary (defined "good enough" threshold)

- separation boundary (archive and role transfer)

- release boundary (explicit decision to stop carrying demand)

When loops remain open, it is usually because one required boundary is missing.

Knowledge Work Loops

Knowledge work loops often stay open because refinement is theoretically infinite.

There is almost always "one more pass."

Typical Open-Loop Pattern

- draft exists

- quality is improving

- no explicit done threshold

- no formal handoff event

High-Leverage Closure Sequence

1. Define deliverable scope in one sentence.

2. Declare version boundary (v1.0, final for this decision cycle).

3. Execute formal handoff with a clear acceptance ask.

4. Archive active artifacts after acceptance.

5. Route future improvements to separate backlog (v2 list).

Example

A strategy memo has seen nine revisions and still feels active.

Closure move:

- declare "decision memo v1.0"

- present to decision owner

- obtain explicit accept/reject

- archive v1 and move enhancements to v2 backlog

Result:

loop closes without pretending the work is eternally perfect.

Creative Work Loops

Creative loops resist closure because identity and output get fused.

People stop asking "Is this complete enough for release?" and ask "Is this me at my absolute best forever?"

That standard prevents closure.

Typical Open-Loop Pattern

- iterative polishing with no public release boundary

- emotional reluctance to finalize

- ongoing private revisions without audience feedback

High-Leverage Closure Sequence

1. Set a release format and date (showing, submission, publication).

2. Define final pass criteria before the pass begins.

3. Complete final pass once.

4. Release publicly or to target recipient.

5. Move all post-release ideas to next-work file, not current artifact.

Example

A creator keeps reworking chapter language for months.

Closure move:

- lock manuscript pass date

- submit to beta readers by deadline

- no edits after submission window closes

- capture future edits in next-edition notes

Result:

creative quality improves through cycles, not endless internal recursion.

Leadership and Management Loops

Leadership loops stay open when decisions are announced but not structurally transferred.

A leader "decides," but ownership and close criteria remain ambiguous.

Typical Open-Loop Pattern

- decision made verbally

- no owner transfer artifact

- no success criteria

- repeated return to same decision in later meetings

High-Leverage Closure Sequence

1. State decision in writing.

2. Assign clear owner and deadline.

3. Define what counts as complete.

4. Publish to affected stakeholders.

5. Schedule review as separate loop, not continuation of decision loop.

Example

A staffing model decision keeps resurfacing every week.

Closure move:

- decision note published with owner matrix

- implementation checkpoint scheduled

- review date framed as new loop with new criteria

Result:

decision loop closes; execution loop begins.

Relational Loops

Relational loops are unique because closure may depend on another person who may not engage.

Waiting for bilateral closure can keep loops open indefinitely.

Typical Open-Loop Pattern

- unresolved conversation replayed mentally

- imagined future resolution holds active demand

- no internal release condition

High-Leverage Closure Sequence

1. Clarify desired resolution in writing.

2. Attempt direct resolution if appropriate and safe.

3. If bilateral closure is unavailable, perform unilateral release.

4. Mark release with a concrete ritual or written declaration.

5. Define re-engagement boundary (if any) moving forward.

Unilateral closure is not denial.

It is recognition that continued loop maintenance has become more costly than continued pursuit.

Learning and Skill-Acquisition Loops

Learning loops commonly remain open because intake is rewarded more than application.

Typical Open-Loop Pattern

- courses, books, notes, frameworks accumulate

- little externalized application

- confidence does not rise despite heavy input

High-Leverage Closure Sequence

1. Define one real-world application task.

2. Execute by a fixed date.

3. Produce visible artifact (demo, memo, training, result).

4. Collect feedback.

5. Close learning loop and open next skill loop.

Learning closes through expression, not additional consumption.

Context-to-Closure Worksheet

For each major loop, fill:

- Context type:

- Missing boundary:

- Selected closure mechanism:

- Closure artifact:

- Completion date:

If a loop remains active after closure attempt, reassess context type first.

Many failed closure attempts are actually context misclassification.

Key Takeaways

- Loop closure is contextual, not one-size-fits-all.

- Open loops persist where boundaries are missing.

- Different domains require different closure artifacts.

- Context-specific closure increases speed and quality simultaneously.

Chapter 12 - Restoring Clean Transitions

Most people manage tasks and ignore transitions.

That is a costly oversight.

A task can be correct and still fail if the transition into or out of that task is unstable.

Transitions are where loop integrity is either protected or lost.

If boundaries are ambiguous, old demands leak into new states.

This chapter provides practical transition design so sequence stays intact under real pressure.

What Transition Failure Looks Like

Common signs:

- finishing work but feeling mentally "still on"

- opening new work and immediately reactivating old unresolved work

- ending days without clear closure boundary

- entering work sessions without clear state intention

When these patterns repeat, people often prescribe better planning.

The actual fix is usually better transitions.

The Three Transition Boundaries

Every clean transition has three components:

1. Exit boundary

Explicitly ends the current state/loop.

2. Neutral boundary

Creates brief non-directional space (Pause) to reduce carryover.

3. Entry boundary

Explicitly starts the next state with clear intention.

Skipping the neutral boundary is the most common error.

Without it, people attempt to shift direction while still carrying prior demand.

Minimal Transition Rituals (Individual)

These are intentionally short so they survive real schedules.

End-of-Work Exit Ritual (3-5 minutes)

1. Write "closed / open" for top three active items.

2. Identify one closure action for each open item.

3. Declare: "Done for today."

4. Physically or digitally close workspace.

Purpose:

prevent unresolved cognitive carryover into non-work time.

Midday State Shift Ritual (2-3 minutes)

1. Name current state.

2. Name intended next state.

3. Write one action that fits next state.

4. Begin only that action.

Purpose:

replace reactive switching with deliberate transition.

Pre-Exhale Entry Ritual (2 minutes)

1. Confirm loop closure status of prerequisite work.

2. Define specific external output for this cycle.

3. Set stop condition ("this Exhale ends when X is delivered").

Purpose:

prevent expression attempts from unresolved or ambiguous starting points.

Team Transition Design

Teams need shared transition cues, not just individual discipline.

Meeting Exit Protocol

Before meeting close, capture:

- decision made

- owner assigned

- done criteria

- next checkpoint

If one of these is missing, the meeting loop often remains open.

Weekly Closure Block

Reserve a fixed block for:

- open-loop review

- closure artifacts

- carry-forward decisions

Do not use this block for new initiative launch.

Mixing launch and closure in the same block weakens both.

Sprint or Cycle Boundary Protocol

At cycle end:

1. close or explicitly defer unfinished work

2. archive closed artifacts

3. list residual open loops with owners

4. open next cycle as a separate loop

This prevents cycle bleed where "next sprint" inherits unresolved ambiguity silently.

Transition Failure Patterns and Fixes

Pattern 1: Hard stop without closure note

Fix: add one-minute closure declaration.

Pattern 2: Constant context switching with no neutral pause

Fix: insert micro-Pause between major directional shifts.

Pattern 3: New work starts before prior loop status is assessed

Fix: require open/closed call before major initiation.

Pattern 4: Team exits meetings without ownership transfer

Fix: enforce owner + acceptance boundary before close.

Designing for High-Pressure Environments

In high-tempo contexts, long rituals usually fail.

Use short, high-reliability cues:

- single-line closure statements

- fixed handoff templates

- standardized end-of-shift transition checklist

The rule is not complexity.

The rule is repeatability under stress.

7-Day Transition Reset

Use this protocol when transition quality is visibly degraded:

Day 1-2:

- install end-of-day exit ritual

Day 3-4:

- install one midday state shift ritual

Day 5-6:

- implement meeting exit protocol with owner transfer

Day 7:

- review friction events; identify where boundaries failed

Keep only what reduces friction measurably.

Key Takeaways

- Transition quality determines whether sequence is preserved.

- Clean transitions require exit, neutral, and entry boundaries.

- Simple rituals outperform complex systems in real conditions.

- Teams need shared closure cues to prevent systemic loop bleed.

Chapter 13 - Teams and Organizations - State-Aware Team Execution

Most teams do not fail from lack of effort.

They fail from poor condition-matching at group scale.

When a team experiences friction, the default response is usually one of these:

- increase accountability pressure

- add status checks

- add process

- accelerate cadence

Sometimes those moves help.

Often they multiply noise.

If the underlying issue is state mismatch or unresolved loop load, additional control pressure creates a busier version of the same problem.

State-aware execution gives teams a simpler path:

diagnose condition first, then match intervention.

The Team-Level Diagnostic Lens

At team level, three structural conditions explain most avoidable drag:

1. Capacity deficit (Inhale problem)

The team is being asked to express beyond current readiness.

2. Transition instability (Pause problem)

Boundaries between planning, execution, and review are collapsed.

3. Residual demand load (open-loop problem)

Unresolved commitments are silently taxing current work.

The right operating question is:

Which condition is dominant this week?

Anti-Pattern: Everything Becomes an Execution Deficit

In many organizations, all friction is interpreted as underperformance.

Signals are flattened:

- missed deadlines -> "ownership issue"

- low velocity -> "urgency issue"

- rework -> "quality issue"

Those labels may be directionally true, but they are incomplete.

They describe outcomes, not causes.

A state-aware team asks one layer deeper:

- Is this output demand exceeding available capacity?

- Are transitions too compressed to stabilize?

- Are open loops contaminating current commitments?

State-Aware Weekly Rhythm (30 Minutes)

Use a fixed weekly sequence:

1. Condition scan (10 minutes)

- Each lead reports one dominant condition: capacity, transition, or loop load.

2. Loop exposure (10 minutes)

- Team identifies the top three unresolved demands causing cross-project drag.

3. Match one intervention per condition (10 minutes)

- Capacity deficit -> adjust load or strengthen Inhale.

- Transition instability -> protect boundary and reduce switching.

- Open-loop load -> close one severe loop before adding major work.

This is not extra bureaucracy.

It replaces low-value debate with condition-specific action.

Team Meeting Prompts That Improve Accuracy

Use short prompts that reinforce structural language:

- "What are we trying to close this week?"

- "What is complete enough to release?"

- "Where are we carrying unresolved demand?"

- "What transition boundary is currently failing?"

- "What work should not be started until a loop is closed?"

Prompt quality shapes diagnosis quality.

Role-Level Responsibilities

Team lead

- call condition first before requesting speed

- protect transition windows

- enforce closure artifacts for critical loops

Individual contributors

- flag unresolved loop load early

- classify blockers structurally, not personally

- confirm open/closed status before accepting new high-load items

Operations/program layer

- track loop inventory trends

- identify recurrent boundary failures

- prevent perpetual initiative stacking

Example: Product Team Under Deadline Compression

Observed:

- velocity down 20%

- rising meeting hours

- delivery slips

Initial response considered:

daily standups + tighter status reporting.

State-aware diagnosis:

- high open-loop load from prior launch decisions

- transition collapse between planning and delivery

- no clear closure boundary on "in progress" initiatives

Intervention:

- close top two severe loops first

- enforce decision-to-owner transfer in writing

- create no-meeting transition block before delivery windows

Four-week effect:

- fewer escalations

- improved on-time release

- lower reported fragmentation without added headcount

Team Metrics That Matter

Instead of tracking activity only, add condition metrics:

- severe open loops per team

- mean time to closure for critical loops

- % meetings ending with owner + done criteria

- number of initiatives launched vs retired per cycle

- transition-protected hours per week

These metrics expose structural load before burnout symptoms appear.

Common Team Errors

Error 1: Mistaking urgency for clarity.

Fix: define closure boundaries before acceleration.

Error 2: Treating transition time as inefficiency.

Fix: protect small neutral buffers to reduce rework.

Error 3: Launching new work to escape unresolved work.

Fix: apply "one severe loop first" rule.

Error 4: Asking for accountability without diagnostic language.

Fix: standardize condition prompts in leadership communication.

Key Takeaways

- Team friction is usually condition failure before it is effort failure.

- State-aware cadence reduces churn without heavy process overhead.

- Closure and transition quality are measurable and manageable.

- Better prompts produce better team diagnosis and better execution.

Chapter 14 - Organizational Loop Hygiene

Organizations create open loops at scale through policy, cadence, and incentive design.

Individuals then absorb that structural load and are told to become more resilient.

That is backwards.

If leadership wants sustainable performance, loop hygiene must be designed into the operating system.

What Systemic Open Loops Look Like

Signs of weak loop hygiene:

- initiatives multiply but rarely retire

- decisions are announced without implementation ownership

- project statuses remain "in progress" indefinitely

- teams repeatedly revisit "settled" topics

- recovery programs expand while fragmentation remains high

These are not isolated management misses.

They are organization-level closure failures.

Four Root Causes

1. Perpetual launch culture

Starting is rewarded more than finishing.

2. Boundary ambiguity

No consistent definition of "done," "accepted," or "closed."

3. Ownership diffusion

Many contributors, no closure authority.

4. Communication overflow

High message velocity with weak transition protocols.

Until these are addressed, local productivity fixes will have limited effect.

Organizational Loop Hygiene Framework

Build hygiene into four layers:

1. Portfolio layer

Every initiative has explicit launch and retirement criteria.

2. Program layer

Every major workstream has owner, closure condition, and handoff protocol.

3. Team layer

Teams run recurring loop review and transition protection rituals.

4. Individual layer

People use state and loop diagnostics to match intervention.

If upper layers are weak, lower layers burn out compensating.

Policy-Level Design Moves

A. Lifecycle governance

Require every initiative to declare:

- purpose

- owner

- success criteria

- closure criteria

- retirement date or review boundary

No closure criteria, no launch approval.

B. Sunset rules

Create default sunset triggers for stale initiatives:

- no measurable progress for defined period

- ownership gap unresolved

- strategic priority change

Sunset decisions close loops and free capacity.

C. Handoff acceptance protocols

A handoff is not complete when sent.

It is complete when accepted by a named receiver with clear next responsibility.

D. Quarterly closure review

Run a dedicated closure review separate from strategy planning.

Goal:

- close, retire, merge, or re-scope unresolved organizational loops.

Do not combine this with new initiative ideation.

Leadership Communication Standards

Leaders can reduce loop creation through language discipline:

- "What does closed look like for this initiative?"

- "Who has acceptance authority?"

- "What are we explicitly retiring this quarter?"

- "What should we stop starting until this closes?"

Language that only emphasizes urgency, volume, or visibility usually increases open-loop load.

Incentives and Performance Systems

Many organizations reward visible activity over resolved value.

Adjust incentives to include:

- closure quality

- handoff reliability

- retirement discipline

- reduction in unresolved cross-team demand

When completion and closure are rewarded differently, closure usually loses.

Design the scorecard so it can win.

Example: Cross-Functional Program Overload

Initial state:

- 19 active initiatives

- most "in progress" > 90 days

- leadership escalation increasing

- burnout interventions underway with little outcome change

Hygiene intervention:

- portfolio triage: close/retire 6 initiatives

- enforce owner + acceptance for remaining initiatives

- quarter-end closure review installed

- no new launch without closure criteria

Result (one quarter):

- active initiative count down

- decision churn reduced

- clearer ownership

- higher on-time completion and lower escalation noise

Implementation Sequence for Executives

Month 1:

- audit open-loop inventory across major functions

- define enterprise closure taxonomy (active, at risk, closed, retired)

Month 2:

- install lifecycle and handoff standards

- train leaders on condition-first review prompts

Month 3:

- run first quarterly closure review

- publish closures and retirements

- align scorecards to closure quality metrics

This sequence creates visible institutional commitment to loop hygiene.

Key Takeaways

- Systemic open loops are an organizational design problem, not an individual weakness.

- Loop hygiene must be embedded in governance, not delegated to personal resilience.

- Closure criteria, ownership, and retirement rules are core operating infrastructure.

- Without institutional closure, burnout initiatives will remain partially effective.

Chapter 15 - 30-Day Implementation Playbook

Frameworks fail in implementation for one reason more than any other: people try to change everything at once.

This playbook is designed to prevent that.

The goal of the first 30 days is not mastery.

The goal is operational traction:

- better diagnosis

- cleaner closure

- more stable transitions

- measurable reduction in fragmentation

Use the plan as written before customizing.

Sequence matters in implementation as much as in the framework itself.

Operating Principles for the 30 Days

1. Diagnose before intervening.

2. Close severe loops before launching major new work.

3. Install small transition rituals that can survive stress.

4. Track outcomes weekly with simple, visible metrics.

Do not add new methods during this 30-day period unless necessary.

You are testing condition-first execution, not stacking tools.

Days 1-7: Diagnose

Objective:

build baseline visibility of state and loop conditions.

Daily actions:

- Run Pause Decision Sequence once per day.

- Score top 1-3 active demands using the 9-item loop check.

- Record one-line classification: Inhale, Pause, Exhale, open/closed.

End-of-week outputs:

- baseline count of severe loops (6+ YES)

- top recurring friction triggers

- most common misclassification pattern

Questions to answer by Day 7:

- Where are you forcing output from depletion?

- Where are you calling open loops "normal workload"?

- Where are transitions most unstable?

Days 8-14: Close

Objective:

convert diagnosis into closure action.

Daily actions:

- Select one high-load open loop.

- Apply one matched closure mechanism.

- Produce closure artifact (handoff note, acceptance message, archive record, version declaration).

Rules:

- one severe loop first

- no new major commitments until one severe loop is closed

- closure without artifact does not count

End-of-week outputs:

- number of loops moved from severe to partial/closed

- mean time from loop identification to closure action

- subjective fragmentation trend (down/same/up)

Days 15-21: Protect Transitions

Objective:

reduce state bleed-through and reactivation noise.

Install at least two rituals:

1. End-of-day exit ritual (3-5 minutes)

2. Weekly closure review block (15-30 minutes)

Optional third ritual:

- pre-Exhale entry cue for high-stakes output sessions

Track:

- how often rituals were executed

- number of friction events tied to boundary failure

- meeting exits with owner + done criteria

End-of-week outputs:

- transition compliance rate

- top boundary failure mode

- one ritual to refine, one ritual to keep unchanged

Days 22-30: Stabilize and Scale

Objective:

lock in what works and remove what creates churn.

Actions:

- review which methods perform better after state-first diagnosis

- remove one forcing behavior that repeatedly violates sequence

- standardize one durable weekly operating rhythm

- document "if/then" playbook for future friction events

Team version:

- include one team-level condition scan in weekly planning

- include one closure metric in team dashboard

- include one retirement/sunset decision in monthly review

End-of-week outputs:

- updated operating playbook (one page)

- retained rituals list

- next-30-day improvement target

Metrics Dashboard (Minimum Viable)

Track these weekly:

- severe open loops (count)

- closure artifact completion (%)

- transition ritual execution (%)

- unresolved carryover items (count)

- perceived fragmentation (1-10)

- recoverability score ("after rest, can I re-enter coherently?" 1-10)

Trend direction matters more than perfect precision.

Common 30-Day Failure Modes

Failure mode 1: Trying to optimize everything in Week 1.

Fix: diagnose first, intervene second.

Failure mode 2: Closing low-risk loops and avoiding severe loops.

Fix: enforce one severe loop first rule.

Failure mode 3: Ritual overload.

Fix: keep only 2-3 small rituals with high adherence.

Failure mode 4: No artifact discipline.

Fix: visible closure proof required.

Failure mode 5: Treating one good week as stable adoption.

Fix: run a second 30-day cycle with tighter metrics.

Applied Example: Solo Operator

Initial state:

- 5 severe loops

- high late-evening cognitive return

- rest not restoring

30-day moves:

- week 1 diagnosis

- week 2 closure of two severe loops via handoff and version split

- week 3 end-of-day closure ritual + weekly review

- week 4 removed overcommitment pattern and retained two rituals

Outcome:

- severe loops reduced from 5 to 2

- lower end-of-day activation

- improved next-morning re-entry quality

Applied Example: 8-Person Team

Initial state:

- multiple cross-functional initiatives with no retirement criteria

- frequent meeting rework

- velocity pressure rising

30-day moves:

- condition scan adopted weekly

- closure artifacts required for top three initiatives

- meeting exit protocol enforced

- one initiative retired to free capacity

Outcome:

- reduced escalation noise

- higher clarity on ownership

- fewer "surprise reopen" decisions

Key Takeaways

- 30-day success is measured by reduced fragmentation and improved recoverability.

- Sequence in implementation prevents framework dilution.

- Closure artifacts and transition rituals are the highest-leverage operational moves.

- Small reliable practices outperform large inconsistent programs.

Conclusion: The Point of the Framework

The promise of this framework is deliberately modest and operational:

better diagnosis before intervention.

Breath State does not claim to solve every performance problem.

It gives you a stable way to identify a class of predictable failures that many people misread:

- mismatch between demanded behavior and active state

- unresolved loop load carried across transitions

- collapsed boundaries that make recovery and execution interfere

When those failures are named correctly, the path forward becomes simpler.

You stop treating structure as character.

You stop prescribing force where closure is required.

You stop confusing activity with progress.

What Changes When State Comes First

When state precedes method:

- effort becomes more proportional to condition

- recovery becomes more functional because unresolved load is addressed

- output quality improves because expression happens from readiness

- teams reduce churn by closing loops instead of escalating noise

This does not eliminate hard work.

It makes hard work coherent.

What This Framework Is Not Trying to Be

It is not a replacement for all planning and execution systems.

It is not a diagnostic model for mental health.

It is not an identity framework.

Its value is narrower and therefore more usable:

it helps you decide what kind of action is structurally appropriate now.

A Practical Commitment

If you adopt one habit from this book, make it this:

Before asking "What should I do next?"

ask "What condition am I in, and is this loop open or closed?"

That question is small.

Its effects are large.

Final Note

Sustainable performance is not built by permanent intensity.

It is built through clean cycles:

accumulate, transition, express, close, recover, repeat.

The framework is only useful if it remains observable in real conditions.

Use it where friction appears.

Use it where your team gets stuck.

Use it where output and recovery are both degrading.

If it helps you reduce unnecessary force and restore reliable movement, it is working.

Appendix A: Canonical Glossary

Inhale: inward accumulation of capacity.

Pause: neutral suspension between directional states; no loops.

Exhale: outward expression producing external effect.

Loop: completion status of Inhale or Exhale.

Closed loop: no residual demand remains active.

Open loop: unresolved demand continues to claim resources.

Friction: diagnostic signal of mismatch or unresolved loop load.

www.ingramcontent.com/pod-product-compliance
Lightning Source LLC
Chambersburg PA
CBHW070814280326
41934CB00012B/3190